Habit Stacking for Entrepreneurs

Using the Power of Habits to Turn Small Challenges into Big Results

Ric Thompson

Ric Thompson

Table of Contents

Introduction

I want to thank you and congratulate you for purchasing the book, *"Habit Stacking for Entrepreneurs, Using the Power of Habits to Turn Small Changes into Big Results."*

Welcome to the exciting new world of habit stacking! If you are looking for ideas on how to make your life and your business as efficient as possible, you have come to the right place. This guide will tell you everything you need to know to use the things you already do every day as springboards to build new, life-improving habits.

Everyone knows that it is difficult to break old habits and build new ones, but most of us don't really understand why. New advances in brain science offer a better understanding of what keeps us from making the big changes we want to make to improve our lives and build our businesses.

Habit stacking is a process that uses this new understanding of what keeps us doing the things we are already doing instead of doing the things we want to be doing and uses it to make real change possible. Everything you need to know to understand about how habit stacking works and to start creating your own habit-stacking routines in contained in this guide.

Thanks for reading!

Ric Thompson

What is Habit Stacking?

Everyone knows that the best way to make changes to your life is to focus on building the kinds of habits that support the life you want. Unfortunately, most of us struggle to eliminate the bad habits and to build the good ones. If you have ever tried to lose weight, quit smoking, eat better, or exercise more, you understand that making big changes is really hard.

And that may actually be the problem.

See, it turns out that our brains are pretty hardwired to keep doing the things we are currently doing. This means that each time we follow a bad habit, we are actually telling our brain it is something we want to do again. Our brain obliges by marking the path that habit took as one "often traveled." This is all well and good, until you remember that our brains do not have an endless amount of resources with which to keep multiple paths clear and operational. This means we lose paths that we aren't using.

Imagine that you have a big yard. There are four paths from the house to the cars. The first time it snows, you might clear all four of those paths because the snow isn't that deep, and you aren't yet tired of snow. However, as storm after storm comes and dumps more snow into that big yard, you start to realize that you are using the same path from the house to the cars every day. Eventually, you will stop clearing those other three paths because they aren't being used, and you are spending a lot of time and energy shoveling them.

This is kind of what happens in your brain. As the frequency with which you use specific paths decreases, your brain stops maintaining them. Eventually they are cut from the list of paths to maintain.

To understand this better, let's look at the science for a minute.

The Science Behind Habit Stacking

A scientific study conducted at Oxford University in England in 2007 found that newborn babies have 41% more neurons than adults on average. You may be thinking that doesn't make any sense since newborn babies haven't really had any experiences yet to start building neurons and the synapses that connect them. The researchers were as surprised as you, so they dug deeper. What they uncovered is the key to being able to build better habits and make the changes to your life that you have been dreaming about.

The research team knew from other studies that as people age, the brain is hard at work keeping things neat and tidy. This means keeping the synapses we use all the time strong and available and pruning the synapses that have fallen into disuse. In essence, this is the reason that practice makes perfect when it comes to learning how to do something new like play the guitar or speak another language. The more you do it, the more primed your brain is to do it again.

Unfortunately, this works as well for the habits we don't like as it does for the ones we want to adopt.

It also helps explain why existing habits are so hard to break and new habits are hard to build. Most importantly, it gives us the key we need to crack the habit problem forever. Instead of trying to make big sweeping changes that allow us to replace a bad habit with a good habit, we need to leverage the habits we already have and use those to build the new ones. This is the basis of habit stacking.

A Hard Habit to Break

To illustrate, let's look at someone who has been trying for years to lose weight unsuccessfully. Generally, when this person embarks on a new weight loss effort, they decide to change almost everything they eat, increase their daily water intake substantially, avoid all the foods they cannot have, and exercise more regularly.

That is a lot of things to try to change at once, especially when you consider that her brain is going to be fighting her the whole time. Her brain wants her to do the same things she always does because those paths are clear and ready to go. It will take a monumental effort to make all those changes at once and to develop and build the new habits and synapses to support them.

So, does this mean we are doomed to do what we have always done, even when it is really bad for us?

Of course not! It just means that trying to make a bunch of big changes all at the same time isn't the right way to go about it. Instead, let's use what we know about how our brain works as a tool to help us succeed rather than fighting against how it works. We know that our brain strengthens the synapses that we use which makes it easy to do these things again and again. So instead of trying to re-route these pathways, let's use them instead. Let's pick a new habit we want to adopt and tie it to a habit we already have. In essence, let's trick our brains into doing something new by making it think it is something old.

That is how habit stacking works.

Habit Stacking, Explained

To illustrate, let's look at an example. John really wants to make sure he gets his eight glasses of water a day, but he has been struggling to remember to choose water instead of coffee or soda. Instead of trying to force his brain to divert the path that currently connects "thirsty" to "soda," John picks a couple daily habits that he already has like brushing his teeth, walking to his favorite lunch spot, and reading his emails before dinner, and decides that after each of those habits he is going to drink a glass of water.

The next morning he gets up, brushes his teeth, and drinks a glass of water. At lunch, he grabs his water bottle and drinks another glass worth of water on the way to get his lunch. When he gets home, he grabs a glass of ice and a bottle of water and sits down to go through his email. Within a few weeks, he doesn't even have to think about drinking more water because he is already doing it as part of those other daily routines.

Back to the Science

So, what does this process of strengthening synapses and building easily traveled pathways have to do with the fact that babies have so many more neurons than adults?

When babies are born, their brains are like a blank slate. Like I said earlier, they don't have any experiences to shape their neurons and synapses. This is why their brains are so full of new neurons; they are all waiting for experiences. It is these experiences that will shape their brain, making some neurons and synapses strong and vibrant, and pruning and removing those that aren't getting used enough.

Adult brains, unfortunately, are the opposite of a blank slate. They are hardwired for certain things. Many of their neurons have been pruned and discarded. The paths that they have are very strong and vibrant, however, and this is why habit stacking works where other attempts to change habits have not. Rather than trying to reroute these pathways or replace them, habit stacking uses them to help you make the changes you want to make.

With that understanding, let's look at how this works in practice.

What is a Habit-stacking routine?

Whether you realize it or not, you use habits everyday in order to do the things you need to do. In fact, many of our strongest habits are things we are hardly aware of anymore because they are so ingrained and so automatic. This includes things like brushing our teeth, taking a shower, and driving to work. We may not even consider these habits, even though they are, especially when it comes to habit stacking. These kinds of habits are the ones that you can use to help you make the changes you want to make.

How Do You Stack Habits?

Now that we understand a little more about what is going on in our brains, we can get into the nuts and bolts of habit stacking and talk about how you do it and why it works.

Think of habit stacking as a way to build on your success. You begin with an ingrained habit like brushing your teeth. It is very likely that you simply do this every morning without having to think about it. Now, let's say you want to do a couple minutes of deep breathing exercises every day. You can stack the new deep breathing habit on top of the ingrained brushing your teeth habit. This basically means that after you brush your teeth, you will do the deep breathing exercises.

By tying them together this way you use the ingrained, reinforced pathway that makes you brush your teeth without thinking about it, to help you add the new habit of doing deep breathing exercises. At first, you will have to remember that after brushing your teeth you do deep breathing, but over time the deep breathing habit will become as ingrained as the brushing your teeth habit.

Stacking More than Two Habits

If you think about it, you are already doing this in several areas of your life. A perfect example is taking a shower in the morning. While it might seem like "showering" is a habit in its own right, it is actually several habits stacked together or a habit-stacking routine. This routine is comprised of several distinct habits like washing your hair, shaving, washing your body, and washing your face. Each of these little habits are stacked atop one another to create the showering routine which you probably do in the same order every day without ever really thinking about what you are doing.

When we begin stacking habits together we are creating habit-stacking routines. These routines can become like habits themselves and they make it easier for us to remember to do each of the individual habits because they are packaged together.

Steps to Building a Habit-stacking routine

Developing habit-stacking routines is at the heart of using this technique to change your life. While you can create whatever kind of routine works for you, there is a formula recommended by many experts that has always worked well for me. Essentially, it provides a repeatable habit you can use to build other habit-stacking routines! In the next few chapters we will look at the steps I use when building my habit-stacking routines.

Step #1: The Ingrained Habit

The first step in developing a new habit-stacking routine is to pick the current habit you can use as the base of the stack. This would be something like brushing your teeth, driving to work, checking your voicemail, or getting changed for bed. It is something you already do without really thinking about it every day.

To find some ingrained habits you can use as the basis for your stack, think about the things you do every day. Start from the minute you wake up in the morning and make a list of all the repetitive things you do. Your list might look something like this:

- Get out of bed
- Brush my teeth
- Shower
- Get dressed
- Make coffee
- Make breakfast
- Take vitamins/medication
- Workout
- Make lunch
- Take kids to school
- Drive to work
- Eat lunch
- Drive home

- Make dinner

- Eat dinner

- Put kids to bed

- Get changed for bed

These are just examples, and your list is likely to be longer than this. Don't worry if you don't capture all the habits you already have in place. The goal is to get you started thinking about what kind of habits you currently use to get things done so that you can identify a few that can serve as the base of your stack.

Once you have a list, look for one or two that you never have to think about that are not constrained in terms of time. For example, taking the kids to school is probably a well-ingrained habit that might seem like the perfect base for a habit stack. However, if you only have enough time between dropping the kids off at school and the start of your work day to make the drive from their school to your work, you won't have time to add any new habits. This means dropping the kids off at school probably isn't a good fit for a base when you are first starting out.

Exercise: Find a Solid Base

If you didn't already, sit down and make a list of all the habits you already use to get through your day. Examine each one to see if it would make a good base. Cross out any that have time constraints or other factors that make them unsuitable. This gives you a list of potential bases on which you can build your first stack.

Step #2: The New Habit

Next, you need to decide what new habit you want to work on adding to your day. Start by thinking of those little things that you always mean to do like drink more water or meditate, that you just never seem to get to. Don't constrain yourself here to things that you should do or that seem possible. At this stage, open your mind to possibility, and brainstorm all the small changes you would love to make that could make a big difference in your life.

To get you thinking, here are some basic ideas:

- Drink water
- Take vitamins
- Stretch
- Go outside
- Call a lead
- Take a deep breath
- Sweep a floor
- Clean a toilet
- Sing a song
- Make a bed
- Eat fruit
- Eat a vegetable
- Do sit-ups
- Meditate

The list of possible habits you want to build is endless and depends completely on your goals and the life you are striving to build. Once you have a couple ideas for the kinds of new habits you want to build, you will need to look them over to make sure they follow the rules of what makes a habit suitable to be included in a stack.

There are eight rules that you should use when developing successful habit-stacking routines. The first four help you pick the right habits, and the other four relate to building out your stacking routine. To start, let's look at the first four; the ones that specifically apply to which kinds of habits work well in habit stacks to give you the basis you need to pick the new habit you want to use in your first stack. The other four will be covered in the next chapter.

There are four rules you should use to determine which new habits can be used in a habit-stacking routine.

Rule #1: Simple

One of the goals of habit stacking is to increase your efficiency, which is why it is critical that any habit you include in your habit-stacking routines is simple. Simple means you can do it almost anywhere, you don't need a bunch of things or people to do it, and it doesn't require any mental or physical preparation on your part. According to this rule, establishing a new habit of doing a deep breathing exercise is suited for habit stacking while going to a yoga class is not.

Rule #2: Life Improving

Any habit you are thinking of adopting should enhance or improve your life in some way. If it doesn't, you should examine why you are seeking to build that behavior into a habit in the first place. For example, spending a few minutes chatting with the other moms when you drop your kids off at school could be a good habit stacking choice if your goal is to make new connections or stay informed. However, if you find that the other moms are gossipy and catty and the reason it is on your list is because it is something you think you should do, it isn't a good habit stacking fit.

Rule #3: Less Than Five Minutes

Choose habits that take less than five minutes to complete from start to finish when deciding which new habits will be a good fit for a habit-stacking routine. This is important because if a habit takes longer than five minutes there is a good chance it violates rule #1 above and/or rule #4 below. Also, choosing habits that take longer than five minutes decreases the number of habits you can add to a stack. If there is a habit that you would really like to add that will take longer than five minutes to do, see if you can get the result you are looking with several small five minute habits rather than one longer thing that takes too much time.

Rule #4: Complete and Concise

As you review your list of potential new habits, you are likely to find that many of them are not "complete" habits. What I mean by "complete" is that the habit is a concise and distinct action that will always be the same. For example, "drink eight ounces of water" is a complete, concise habit and once you develop it, it will always be the same. "Eat more fruit" is not a concise habit because more is ambiguous. If you changed it to "eat a piece of fruit," it becomes complete and concise. Likewise, "do five minutes of housework" is not a complete habit, because what kind of housework you are doing changes every day. In order for the habit stacking process to work, you need to pick concise, complete habits to create your stack.

Exercise: Pick the Right Habits

If you didn't already, take a few minutes to create a list of all the new habits you would like to build. Don't limit yourself when making the list. Write down all the things you would like to change. Once you have your list, go back through and consider each habit carefully. Does it follow the rules? If it doesn't, can it be broken down into smaller pieces that follow the rules? Eliminate any habits that don't follow the rules above, and you will be left with a list of potential new habits that you can use to create your first stacking routine.

Step #3: Creating the Routine

You should now have a list of potential existing habits that can form the base of your habit-stacking routine and a list of new habits you want to develop that should work within a habit-stacking routine. The next step is to put the two together in a logical way and start building your first habit stack. In order to do that, we need to go over the other rules for creating successful habit-stacking routines.

Rule #5: Logical Flow

In order to give yourself the best possible chance of success, you need to build habit-stacking routines that have a logical flow from one habit to another. This doesn't mean that the habits have to be related to one another. The logical flow has more to do with time, place, and where you are mentally.

For example, let's say you choose brushing your teeth as the base habit you want to build on, and you are trying to decide which of your new habits would be a good fit. You have three potential new habits – eat a piece of fruit, call a lead, and take 10 deep breaths. Start by thinking about what time it is when you are brushing your teeth. Odds are it is first thing in the morning, which means it probably isn't the best time to call a lead. This leaves two options on the table.

Next, think about where you are physically located when you finish brushing your teeth. Since you are probably in the bathroom, eating a piece of fruit might not be a good fit since the fruit is in the kitchen, and for sanitary reasons, most people don't like eating in the bathroom. Also, since you did just brush your teeth, eating anything in the next five minutes is probably not the best fit. This leaves taking 10 deep breaths.

Once you get down to the habit or habits that work from a timing and physical location perspective, it is time to pair each remaining new habit with your existing base habit to see if there is a logical flow from one to the other for you. This step is somewhat subjective since it depends on your mental state and preferences. The key is to look for two habits that flow together in a way that won't be jarring. In our example, taking 10 deep breaths seems to flow well from brushing your teeth. However, if the remaining habit we had was to use a phone app to learn three new vocabulary words, which could work from a time and place perspective, the flow between that and brushing your teeth might not feel logical at all.

You can determine the logical flow for you by considering each possible pairing and picking the one that feels the most logical to you.

Exercise: Find Logical Pairings

Take your list of existing habits, and pick the one you want to use for your first stack. Now look at the list of potential new habits, and run each through the process outlined above to determine which pairs seem logical. You may end up with more than one logical pair, which is fine at this stage. If you get to the point where none of your potential habits seem like a logical fit with the base habit you have chosen, go back and pick another base habit, and go through the process again.

Rule #6: Habit-Stacking Routines Must Be 30 Minutes or Less

The whole point of habit stacking is to help increase the chances of success in building and developing new habits. However, there is a limit to how many new habits you can stack on an old one without compromising this goal. The simple truth is that you can only stack so many new habits onto an existing habit before you lose the benefit of that initial existing habit. For most people, this limit is about 30 minutes of total time spent on a single routine. This means that a complete stack is likely to have six to 15 habits in it if you are following the rules for what makes a habit a good fit for stacking.

In some cases, you may have less than six habits in a complete stack. This can happen if your base habit takes longer than five minutes to complete like showering or going for a 15-minute walk after dinner. It can also happen if you have a limited time frame surrounding your base habit. For example, let's say you are building on taking your morning shower. You may only have 20 minutes between when you get in the shower and when you need to start getting your kids ready for school. If it takes you 10 minutes to shower, you only have time for two new habits in the time you have available. This can also happen if you only have two or three new habits that flow logically from your base habit.

It is important to understand that while you don't want to exceed 30 minutes for a single habit-stacking routine, you don't have to build out each routine to the full 30 minutes if there is a reason not to do so.

Exercise: Identify All the Habits for Your Routine

Once you have two habits, a base habit (1) and a new habit (2), you have a stack. To build on that stack, use your list of new habits and the process above to choose other new habits that have a logical flow from the new habit you have already identified (2) to the next new habit (3). Repeat this process until you have a full stack. Remember, a full stack should never take more than 30 minutes to complete.

Rule #7: Habit-Stacking Routines Have to Fit In Your Life

Of all the rules used to create successful habit-stacking routines, this is the most important. If the habit-stacking routine doesn't fit into your life, it won't work, period.

The process outlined so far is designed to help you develop habit-stacking routines that will fit into your life. However, as everyone knows, how we think things will happen and how they actually happen can be quite different. You may think that it only takes you 10 minutes to take a shower even though you consistently spend at least 20 minutes bathing each morning. You may think it will take you less than five minutes to do 50 sit-ups only to realize you are not quite in good enough shape to do them that quickly. There are many reasons why the reality of our habit-stacking routine won't match our expectations and assumptions.

Since it is critical to your success that your habit-stacking routines fit into your life, you need to take the time to test them out before finalizing them. There are a couple different ways you can do this. The first, which is also the way I am going to recommend you get started with habit stacking later in this guide, is to build out your stack one habit at a time. Rather than trying to add the whole stack of new habits at once, you start with the first new habit (2) and add it to your base habit (1). If you find that the new habit (2) consistently takes five minutes or less and seems to flow logically from the base habit (1), it is a good fit, and you can move on to the next habit in your stack. If at any point in this process you find a habit that doesn't flow or doesn't fit, you can make any necessary changes to that part of the stack without losing the progress you have already made.

The other way to test your stack is to try it out for a couple days and keep track of how things go. You may find that things take more or less time than you expected or that the flow is better or worse than you thought it would be. As you test it out, you can make changes to the order of the new habits in the stack and even swap habits in and out until you find a stack that follows the rules and feels logical to you.

Exercise: Test Your Stack

Pick one of the methods above and start testing out your new habit-stacking routine. Make sure you keep track of how long individual habits are taking to complete and how you feel about the flow of the overall routine so that you can make any necessary adjustments. Once you feel like you have a solid stack, do the exercise under Rule #8 before finalizing your habit-stacking routine.

Rule #8: Habit-Stacking Routines Must Have a Checklist

The final piece of the habit-stacking puzzle is the checklist. To some people, this might seem like overkill or an unnecessary step, but I have found it to be one of the deciding factors between those who use habit stacking to successfully make big changes by changing little things and those who try and fail.

The point of the checklist is to help you quickly move through the habits in your stack without having to think about it and without forgetting any habits. Remember, the goal is to use that existing pathway and repetition to turn the new habits in the stack into ingrained habits. This works best and fastest when you are doing things the same way in the same order every time. Checklists help you do this.

The final step in creating a new habit-stacking routine is to create or finalize the checklist that accompanies it. Depending on how you choose to test your habit stack, it may be beneficial to create a checklist at the start of the testing process. For those who are testing their entire stack at once, using a draft checklist will help you remember to do each habit in order. This can be very beneficial if you are tweaking the stack as you test it. For those who are testing one habit at a time, you can build your checklist as you build your stack.

Eventually, the new habits will become ingrained enough that you won't need the checklist anymore but increase your chances of success by creating a checklist, using it as long as you need to, and then keeping it in a visible place to serve as a reminder even if you don't need to reference it every day.

Exercise: Create a Checklist for Your Routine

Take a few minutes to create a checklist for your habit stack on your computer so that you can print it out multiple times and use it to track your progress every day. Include the amount of time you expect each habit to take on your checklist.

Using Habit-Stacking Routines to Build a Better Life

Now that you understand the steps involved in developing a habit-stacking routine, let's look at some examples of how habit-stacking routines can improve different areas of your life.

Personal Care Habit-Stacking Routines

There are very few people who wouldn't benefit from taking better care of themselves, which is why I chose this area to tackle first. I have also found that entrepreneurs are often the worst when it comes to taking care of themselves and their own needs. To show you how habit stacking can use small changes to create big results, here are some sample habit-stacking routines centered on personal care.

Jumpstart the Day Morning Routine

Base Habit: Getting out of bed	Time: 1 minute
Habit #2: Make the bed	Time: 3 minutes
Habit #3: Drink eight ounces of water	Time: 5 minutes
Habit #4: Take vitamins	Time: 1 minute
Habit #5: Start Coffee	Time: 2 minutes
Habit #6: Do back Stretches for 5 minutes	Time: 5 minutes

Habit #7: Do 50 sit-ups   Time: 10 minutes

Total Time: 27 minutes

Start Out Positive and Peaceful Daily Routine

Base Habit: Brush teeth   Time: 3 minutes

Habit #2: Take 10 deep   Time: 2 minutes
breaths

Habit #3: Meditate for five   Time: 5 minutes
minutes

Habit #4: Write 5 positive   Time: 5 minutes
things in your journal

Habit #5: Say Daily Positive   Time: 2 minutes
Affirmations

Habit #6: Visualize yourself   Time: 5 minutes
having a great day

Habit #7: Send a positive   Time: 2 minutes
text to three people

Total Time: 24 minutes

Looking Your Best Daily Routine

Base Habit: Showering   Time: 15 minutes

Habit #2: Fix your hair   Time: 5 minutes

Habit #3: Check and clip/file nails   Time: 5 minutes

Habit #4: Get dressed   Time: 4 minutes

Habit #5: Check appearance in mirror   Time: 1 minute

Total Time: 30 minutes

Bedtime Daily Routine

Base Habit: 30 mins until bedtime   Time: 0 minute

Habit #2: Take melatonin   Time: 1 minute

Habit #3: Drink a cup of herbal tea   Time: 2 minutes

Habit #4: Brush and Floss Teeth   Time: 5 minutes

Habit #5: Meditate for 5 minutes   Time: 5 minutes

Habit #6: Write in journal   Time: 5 minutes

Habit #7: Write out any thoughts plaguing your mind	Time: 5 minutes
Habit #8: Turn on sound machine, dim lights	Time: 1 minute

Total Time: 24 minutes

Building Your Business Habit-Stacking Routines

As entrepreneurs, the most important thing in your life most of the time is your business. This is a place where developing habit-stacking routines can really pay off in the short and long term. To demonstrate how habit stacking can turn small changes to big benefits in your business, here are some sample habit-stacking routines centered on building your business.

Start Your Day Right Routine

Base Habit: Arrive at the Office	Time: 0 minute
Habit #2: Review your daily schedule	Time: 3 minutes
Habit #3: Check email	Time: 5 minutes
Habit #4: Check voicemail	Time: 3 minutes
Habit #5: Return one phone call	Time: 5 minutes
Habit #6: Call or email one lead	Time: 5 minutes

Habit #7: Get coffee or tea   Time: 2 minutes

Habit #8: Make a list of daily goals   Time: 5 minutes

Habit #9: Organize your desk   Time: 2 minutes

Total Time: 30 minutes

Building Your Business Routine

Base Habit: Return From   Time: 0 minute
Lunch

Habit #2: Call or email one   Time: 5 minutes
Lead

Habit #3: Call or email one   Time: 5 minutes
lead

Habit #4: Follow-up with   Time: 3 minutes
one new contact

Habit #5: Return two   Time: 5 minutes
phone calls

Habit #6: Ask one   Time: 5 minutes
customer for feedback

Habit #7: Brainstorm one   Time: 1 minute
thing you can do better

Habit #8: Review recent   Time: 5 minutes
marketing results

Total Time: 29 minutes

Productivity Boost Routine #1

Base Habit: Afternoon Slump	Time: 0 minute
Habit #2: Go for a five minute walk outside	Time: 5 minutes
Habit #3: Stretch your major muscles	Time: 5 minutes
Habit #4: Take 10 deep breaths	Time: 3 minutes

Total Time: 13 minutes

Productivity Boost Routine #2

Base Habit: Stuck and Feeling Unproductive	Time: 0 minute
Habit #2: Meditate for 5 minutes	Time: 5 minutes
Habit #3: Call someone you love	Time: 5 minutes
Habit #4: Take 10 deep breaths	Time: 3 minutes

Total Time: 13 minutes

Networking Event Routine

Base Habit: Arrive at Networking Event	Time: 0 minute
Habit #2: Scan the room for someone you know	Time: 1 minutes
Habit #3: Make contact with someone you know	Time: 5 minutes
Habit #4: Introduce yourself to new person #1	Time: 1 minutes
Habit #5: Connect with new person #1	Time: 5 minutes
Habit #6: Introduce yourself to new person #2	Time: 1 minutes
Habit #7: Connect with new person #2	Time: 5 minutes
Habit #8: Introduce yourself to new person #3	Time: 1 minutes
Habit #9: Connect with new person #3	Time: 5 minutes
Habit #10: Say Goodbye to #3	Time: 1 minutes
Habit #11: Say Goodbye to #2	Time: 1 minutes

Habit #12: Say Goodbye to #1	Time: 1 minutes
Habit #13: Say Goodbye to the person you know	Time: 1 minute

Total Time: 28 minutes

Overall Wellbeing Habit-Stacking Routines

Even if most of your focus and attention is on building and maintaining your business, you have to pay attention to the other areas of your life so you don't burn out. Creating habit-stacking routines for these areas can really help you ensure that you are devoting time to the other parts of your life which is something many entrepreneurs struggle to do. To help you understand how you can use habit stacking to use small changes in order to achieve big results across your life, here are some sample habit-stacking routines centered on helping you stay connected to the other parts of your life.

Mental Boost Habit-stacking Routines

Base Habit: Finish Dinner	Time: 0 minute
Habit #2: Read a news article	Time: 5 minutes
Habit #3: Call a friend to check in	Time: 5 minutes
Habit #4: Go for a quick walk	Time: 5 minutes

Habit #5: Learn five new   Time: 5 minutes
words in Spanish

Habit #6: Do a crossword   Time: 5 minutes
puzzle for five minutes

Total Time: 25 minutes

Physical Fitness Routine

Base Habit: Arrive home   Time: 0 minutes
from work

Habit #2: Change into   Time: 1 minutes
exercise clothes

Habit #3: Cardio warm-up   Time: 5 minutes
(jogging, jumping jacks)

Habit #4: Stretch major   Time: 5 minutes
muscles

Habit #5: Do 25 squats   Time: 3 minutes

Habit #6: Do 20 pushups   Time: 2 minutes

Habit #7: Do 20 sit-ups   Time: 3 minutes

Habit #8: Do arm reps with   Time: 5 minutes
weights

Habit #9: Run up and down   Time: 2 minutes
the stairs twice

Habit #10: Stretch major muscles	Time: 2 minutes

Total time: 28 minutes

Healthy Diet Daily Habit-stacking Routines

Base Habit: Eat Breakfast	Time: 5 minutes
Habit #2: Pack your lunch	Time: 5 minutes
Habit #3: Pack snacks for the day	Time: 2 minutes
Habit #4: Check meal plan for dinner	Time: 1 minute
Habit #5: Pull dinner ingredients from freezer	Time: 2 minutes
Habit #6: Drink a cup of herbal tea	Time: 5 minutes

Total time: 20 minutes

Emotional Wellness Habit-stacking Routine

Base Habit: Finish eating lunch	Time: 0 minute
Habit #2: Call a friend or family member to chat	Time: 5 minutes

Habit #3: Take 10 deep breaths

Time: 2 minutes

Habit #4: Go for a quick walk outside

Time: 5 minutes

Habit #5: Sit outside and listen to music

Time: 5 minutes

Habit #6: Text three friends or loved ones

Time: 5 minutes

Habit #7: Think of three positive things about today

Time: 3 minutes

Habit #8: Take 10 deep breaths

Time: 2 minutes

Total time: 27 minutes

Conclusion

I hope you found the my guide to habit stacking helpful and that it provided you with the information you need to improve your efficiency and start creating the life you want.

This guide provided you with the know-how you need to identify the right habits to build off of, figure out which habits are suitable for stacking, and create habit-stacking routines that have the best chance of success.

With the information and exercises provided in this guide, you now know:

- What habit stacking is

- How science backs up the idea of habit stacking

- Why it is so hard to build and break habits

- How stacking habits works

- What existing habits make good base habits

- How to determine if a new habit is suitable for stacking

- A step by step process for building a habit-stacking routine

- The rules to follow when creating habit stacks

- How to test your habit-stacking routine

- Why checklists are an important part of the habit-stacking process

- How habit stacking can be used in different parts of your life

From helping you understand why stacking new habits on existing habits makes building new habits easier to providing you with actionable exercises to teach you to make your own stacks, this book provides you with the in-depth information you need to start turning small changes into big results!

Good Luck!

Ric

Check out some of Ric's other books!!

http://www.amazon.com/dp/B00I3Q2QPK

http://www.amazon.com/dp/B00LIGKRCG

http://www.amazon.com/dp/B00H4HHY56

http://www.amazon.com/dp/B00L9K6928

http://www.amazon.com/dp/B00NRVWE3A

http://www.amazon.com/dp/B00O170KVC

www.ingramcontent.com/pod-product-compliance
Lightning Source LLC
Chambersburg PA
CBHW070720180526
45167CB00004B/1549